Big Cats

Tigers

by Marie Brandle

Bullfrog Books

Ideas for Parents and Teachers

Bullfrog Books let children practice reading informational text at the earliest reading levels. Repetition, familiar words, and photo labels support early readers.

Before Reading

- Discuss the cover photo. What does it tell them?
- Look at the picture glossary together. Read and discuss the words.

Read the Book

- "Walk" through the book and look at the photos. Let the child ask questions. Point out the photo labels.
- Read the book to the child, or have him or her read independently.

After Reading

- Prompt the child to think more. Ask: What did you know about tigers before reading this book? What more would you like to learn about them?

Bullfrog Books are published by Jump!
5357 Penn Avenue South
Minneapolis, MN 55419
www.jumplibrary.com

Library of Congress Cataloging-in-Publication Data

Names: Brandle, Marie, 1989– author.
Title: Tigers / by Marie Brandle.
Description: Minneapolis, MN: Jump!, Inc., [2021]
Series: Big cats | Includes index.
Audience: Ages 5–8 | Audience: Grades K–1
Identifiers: LCCN 2020023913 (print)
LCCN 2020023914 (ebook)
ISBN 9781645277316 (hardcover)
ISBN 9781645277323 (ebook)
Subjects: LCSH: Tiger—Juvenile literature.
Classification: LCC QL737.C23 B7249 2021 (print)
LCC QL737.C23 (ebook) | DDC 599.756—dc23
LC record available at https://lccn.loc.gov/2020023913
LC ebook record available at https://lccn.loc.gov/2020023914

Editor: Eliza Leahy
Designer: Michelle Sonnek

Photo Credits: Eric Isselee/Shutterstock, cover, 1, 3, 8, 24; jeep2499/Shutterstock, 4; ewastudio/iStock, 5, 23bl; Juan Carlos Munoz/Shutterstock, 6–7, 23tr; Sourabh Bharti/Shutterstock, 9, 23tl; Setta Sornnoi/Shutterstock, 10–11; Michal Varga/Shutterstock, 12–13; Petr Masek/Shutterstock, 14, 23bm; Kenneth Lawrence/Shutterstock, 15, 23br; Fuse/Getty, 16–17; mauritius images GmbH/Alamy, 18–19, 23tm; Arindam Bhattacharya/Alamy, 20–21.

Printed in the United States of America at Corporate Graphics in North Mankato, Minnesota.

Table of Contents

Black Stripes

What big cats love water?
Tigers!

This tiger lives in a jungle.

Tigers live in dens.
Some are in caves.
Neat!

den

stripe

Tigers have orange fur.
They have black stripes.

The stripes blend in.
This helps tigers hunt.
Cool!

Tigers have big teeth.

Roar!

tooth

claw

Their claws are sharp.
They help tigers hunt, too.

See the padded paws?
They help tigers walk quietly.

paw

They make
big tracks.

track

15

Tigers can jump far.

How far?

About 32 feet
(10 meters).

That is the length
of two cars!

cub

Cubs play tag.
Why?
They learn to hunt!

They go for a swim.

Fun!

Where in the World?

Tigers live in Asia. They can live in many habitats, including mangrove forests, jungles, and grasslands. Take a look!

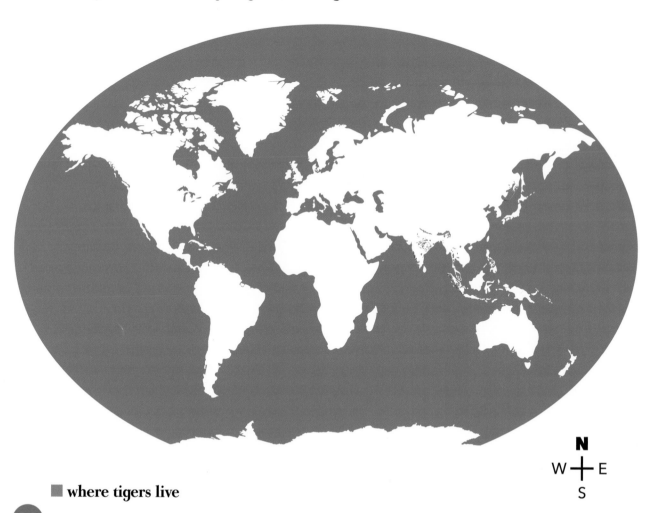

■ where tigers live

Picture Glossary

blend
To mix in with another so that the two things combine together.

cubs
Young tigers.

dens
The homes of wild animals.

jungle
A forest in a tropical area that is covered in thick trees, vines, and bushes.

padded
Cushioned with a soft part on the bottom.

tracks
Marks left behind by moving animals.

Index

To Learn More

Finding more information is as easy as 1, 2, 3.

❶ Go to www.factsurfer.com

❷ Enter "tigers" into the search box.

❸ Choose your book to see a list of websites.